When Mine Canaries Stop Singing

poems by

Nancy Avery Dafoe

Finishing Line Press
Georgetown, Kentucky

When Mine Canaries Stop Singing

Copyright © 2024 by Nancy Avery Dafoe
ISBN 979-8-88838-631-6 First Edition
All rights reserved under International and Pan-American Copyright Conventions. No part of this book may be reproduced in any manner whatsoever without written permission from the publisher, except in the case of brief quotations embodied in critical articles and reviews.

ACKNOWLEDGMENTS

I would like to express my gratitude to my husband Daniel who encouraged this project in the face of my initial doubts about people accepting responsibility for our planet; to my beta readers Priscilla Berggren Thomas, Pen Women Mary Gardner, Judith McGinn, and Janine DeBaise; to my always encouraging daughters Colette and Nicole; and to poets Martin Willitts, Jr. and Bobbie Dumas Panek who wrote back cover endorsements for this collection.

"Chasing Light," "Take the Beaver," and "It's Getting Hotter" appeared in the September 26, 2022 Poetry Showcase of online journal and blog *Fevers of the Mind*, edited by David O'Nan. "Bodies Keep Turning Up," "By the Numbers," "We Better Write About Trees," and "One Day's Headlines: July 20, 2022" (published in an earlier version under the title "A Single Day's Headline,") first appeared in the anthology *Earth Care*, edited by Martin Willitts, Jr. "We Who Are So Concerned with Death" first appeared in *What We See on Our Journeys*, an anthology of poetry by Onondaga County poets, edited by Martin Willitts, Jr. "Language Like Water" first appeared in my chapbook *Poets Diving in the Night* (FLP, 2017). "Hope for Water Bears" appeared in my poetry book *Innermost Sea* (FLP, 2018). Another version of "Things the Water Carried" and an earlier version of "Recalling Blind Beach" were published in my collection *Innermost Sea*. "Corporeal Ghost" first appeared in my chapbook *Poets Diving in the Night*.

Note from the cover artist Katie Turner:

Working in watercolor and with various unusual shape-making tools allows me to explore calligraphic lines, shape and depth in my paintings. This painting is experimental for me as my process incorporates words and line into the intuitive composition. I enjoy the challenge and excitement of combining emotional stories with the developing composition. For me, this painting, Lament, is all about the experience of the profound passion of deep sorrow. There are layers and levels of this passionate expression just like we experience with certain music or poetry. Here I explore to ultimately create an emotional story.

Publisher: Leah Huete de Maines
Editor: Christen Kincaid
Cover Art: Katie Turner
Author Photo: Parker Stone
Cover Design: Elizabeth Maines McCleavy

Order online: www.finishinglinepress.com
also available on amazon.com

Author inquiries and mail orders:
Finishing Line Press
PO Box 1626
Georgetown, Kentucky 40324
USA

Contents

Preface .... *xi*
Briefly Winged 1
Take the Beaver 2
It's Getting Hotter 3
Chasing Light 4
More Than Seven Wonders 5
Our Blue Water Planet is Burning 7
Listen to the Girl 9
Stranded on a Rooftop, Shivering 10
Language Like Water 11
Corporeal Ghost 14
We Had Better Write About Trees 15
Without Ospreys 16
Earth Awakens 17
Examining My Carbon Footprint 18
We Who Are So Concerned with Death 20
Recalling Blind Beach 21
By the Numbers 23
Where Hope Resides 24
A Nursery Rhyme Signal 25
Bodies in Barrels Keep Turning Up 26
Discordant Chorus 27
A River Still Runs Through It 28
Arbiter of Justice 29
Hope for Water Bears 30
Birdlike Bones and Other Assorted Similes 31
Last Light 32
Things the Water Carried 33
When the World Was Young 35
Aliens 37
Once Fallen on Earth 38
Halfway Between the Center and Edge,
   in a Galaxy Called the Milky Way 39

"We exist no longer than mayflies between Heaven and Earth."
Su Shih

Jo Harjo asks us to remember:
our skin is the skin of the earth,
our tribe is the tribe of all animals.
We do well to remember.

Preface

One Day's Headlines: July 20, 2022

Extreme heat prompts alerts in 28 states as Texas, Oklahoma hit 115 ● Air conditioning has a climate problem ● Britain Breaks Temperature Record as Fires Spread Across Europe ● Europe's Heat Wave Shatters British Records and Drives Wildfires ● The U.S. is sweltering ● War and Warming Upend Global Energy Supplies and Amplify Suffering ● Fires Destroy Homes in Greater London ● Sinkhole Swallows Van in the Bronx ● Brutal heat dome moves east, with Central Europe sweltering ● Extreme heat piles on Europe's travel chaos ● Scenes of Devastation From a Fire-Ravaged Southwestern France ● ISIS Fighters' Children Are Growing Up in a Desert Camp ● Europe's heat wave hits U.K. with its hottest day ever ● President Biden to Declare National Climate Emergency ● Famine by October? Somalia & East Africa Face Humanitarian Crisis Amid Climate Change ● Billionaire Fueled Climate Denials ● Feds, Local Governments To Prep For Growing Extreme Heat Threats ● London hits 104 degrees ● Grim warnings are issued as oppressive heat wave in US shows no signs of slowing ● 100 Million Americans Face Dangerous Heat Wave ● Oil exports resume after lengthy hiatus

Briefly Winged

Flight of a single day
is the lifespan of adult mayfly—
with its translucent tall wings
like segmented, painted glass
and its cerci, those three long,
slender, curving "tails" following
in its wake across waters.

Paradox of the ephemeral,
mayfly's claims to immortality
come into play as oldest
winged insect with allusions
to and symbols of brief lifespan
found in nearly every religion:
resurrection. Imprint of its ethereal,
triangular appendages engraved
in rock 300 million years old.

Foretelling health of systems
and life running through water,
these winged creatures hold onto
their ancestral traits, feed all manner
of birds and numerous humans, as well.

Yet something has happened
to the mayfly like the butterfly, too,
something dramatic in their transitory
elegance: their hatches only now
silently trailing
away.

Take the Beaver

Take the beaver, for example,
that industrious, sleek brown creature
slowing rivers, creating wetlands
absorbing toxins; busy beavers building
dams and lodges for their kits nestled
inside lodges with eating chambers
and underwater exits and entrances;
beavers with architecture so intricate, yet
with lives not worth their pelts to man.

Man took the beaver and took
the beaver until that animal
was nearly eradicated, casualty
of fur trade in the making of hats.
Man changed water levels, broke dams,
so, beavers abandoned their lodges
replaced by human genius in carving up
bogs, filling swamps with toxic landfills
leaching into rivers and streams.

Mankind's busy labors sped up water
like high-speed trains for hydroelectricity,
destroying carbon sinks once the domain
of the beaver now in industrial development,
as carbon chokes life, but at least we
have fewer reminders of a simpler time.

A single, loud crack is the water slap
of warning, beaver reminding us:
broad flat tail her instrument.
Reddish-brown guard hairs and natural oils
repel water on her back, keeping inner fur
soft and warm. Her long claws hold a stick
she will push and carry to the lodge she built
where her kits wait: life struggling on
in the face of sophisticated human
systems of waste and ruin.

It's Getting Hotter

It's getting hotter across the planet,
and grasses have turned sizzling brown
as if to please a blistering sun with their burning.

While an ominous shadow crosses the plains
without releasing its rains—that bounty
saved for the terrain where rains are yet plentiful
and creeks and rivers swell until
overflowing, flooding everything
downstream, taking all that is left
of good soil, as elsewhere,
another desert forms.

Icebergs disappearing from warming
realm as ocean temperatures rise,
and cities along the coasts imagine
dikes that will hold back the rising.

Earth is getting hotter,
and all of mankind is moving,
constantly moving in progress
toward conflict and desolation.
Another people in forced migration
on a widening path under cover of night
when it is still cool enough to walk,
with their few belongings on their backs,
across barren lands toward dubious,
distant desire; toward imagined plenty,
they walk, not knowing:

even the stars would reduce
all to ash before they got close.

Chasing Light

Chasing light,
we ran through tall grasses—
my brothers and I wrapped our fingers
around fireflies sending signals in the night.

Before opening our small fists
and releasing those living lanterns,
we imagined life as fairy constellations
mirrored in the bones of our wrists

like Nemerov suggested in his poem *Writing*,
our lives stretched out before us, seemingly infinite
because we were not yet able to imagine death
of ourselves or other species in a flash of light.

More Than Seven Wonders

For sheer magnificence, consider the Bengal tiger
or leap of the snow leopard across a wide chasm.
Be amazed at the scope and disappearance
of the mighty Colossus of Rhodes,
but do not forget the immensity and fertility
of the Great Barrier Reef or the spectacular
darting of red-throated hummingbird.

While human architecture is astonishing,
weed-like protrusions of the leafy sea dragon
are both stunning and practical in camouflaging.
Manufactured scarves of nearly infinite variety
cause pause, but consider the silky blond setae—
fur covering the legs and claws of Yeti Crabs,
known only since 2005, as humans continue
to discover diverse creatures on this blue planet.

By all means, ponder the Great Pyramid of man,
Beethoven's Symphony No. 5, and Shakespeare's
King Lear, but did you know the sloth
can hold its breath for 40 minutes under water?
The sperm whale can dive 9,000 straight down
for its prey and makes the loudest recorded sound
of any creature? Take into account, the agility
in the nearly 300-degree head movement
of the barn owl and bizarre pointed snout
of goblin sharks which can pull their jaws
out of their mouths. Do wonder
at the semi-aquatic Platypus that defies
our neat categorization, or the transparent
hydroid jellyfish with its 90 tentacles
and red stomach showing from its insides out.
Oh, and the eyes of the Aye-Aye, a primate
once killed by men because its penetrating stare
was considered a "bad omen."

Never fail to mention Picasso's art
or the works of Van Gogh and Frida Kahlo, but
for color alone, stop and take in streaking clouds

partially covering a setting sun
with the sky pulsing in that lifeblood.
Be aware of sunset moths of Madagascar
and the rim of the Grand Canyon, along which
bright vermillion, chocolate layers sandwich
greens and yellows beneath variegated yarns
created in the lines of other geologic ages.

While man's monuments—too often built
with slave labor—are awe-inspiring to see,
it would be wise to put them in perspective
and offer nature's versions of our light shows
by witnessing the Northern Lights or
Iguazu Falls for power and beauty.

Failing to mention Glaucus Atlanticus
or blue dragon snail—with its penetrating
color and appendages ending in
bursts of stars—would be a crime.

Peacock spider, this newly discovered Arthropod,
of the genus Maratus, wearing a bright blue mask
with orange stripes on its body is wondrous
to behold. Electric eels, banded armadillos,
and the flightless Kakapo are on our list.
Star-nosed mole, and Christmas tree worm
with spiraling tentacles that breathe wonders.
Tentacles that breathe!

And, of course, the amazingly indestructible
Tardigrades, those micro creatures
most likely to outlive us all.

Our Blue Water Planet is Burning

Our blue water planet is burning.
Our politics are rife with hate, racism, misogyny,
cruelty toward humans, animals, plants;
even rocks have no safeguard once in human sights.
Empathy and sympathy are as endangered
as the elephant and most species.

Turning to the sky—
out beyond darkness of man's constructs—
beyond points of light of a passing aircraft,
beyond rotating satellites and space junk,
beyond what the naked eye is capable
of taking in, there is extraordinary beauty
observed through Chandra's X-ray telescope,
sending images of other worlds, other universes,
triplet black holes, quasars, 3D visualizations
through computer simulations,
oh, and a neutron star pulling in matter:
Dr. Jekyll and Mr. Hyde-named pair
of star and black hole.

Otherness, impossible possible, seen
from our finite position and limited view
made nearly limitless.

Cartwheel Galaxy, 150,000 light years in diameter—
as if we could conceive such expanse
from across our rooms dwarfed
on a blue burning body in the cosmos.

There is the ultraviolent Helix Nebula,
stellar system Eta Carinae—that volatile system
with two massive stars five million times more luminous
than our sun; Supernova 1987A, we are only viewing
after death of that star, its spectacular million-years-ending
looking like alien fireworks in display
of colors, lights, and patterns.

Our minds drawn to beautiful rings of hot gas
spreading across galaxies as interstellar clouds
move across time and space,
limitless to the man or woman standing
at the top of staircase become mountain.

Space not black after all, not empty,
but eternal in eruptions of light and matter—
forever beginning anew.

Listen to the Girl

Listen to the girl,
all 4 feet 7 inches
of that sharp-tongued, Swedish activist
who stands up to political leaders
as if she is ten feet tall holding her sign,
Skolstrejk för klimatet,
and from her unwavering voice,
"How dare you?"

Even at the age of eight,
Greta Thunberg could not understand
why so little was being done
to help the planet,
so she jumped into the fray,
living by her word
as she asks each of us to do.

Listen to the girl.

And from her protest actions
outside the doors: her country's Parliament,
before the United Nations' Climate Conference,
before the UN Climate Action Summit—
a movement grows.

Listen to the girl.

Fridays for Future, described
by activists as the "Greta effect,"
in fact, a demonstration that even one
young voice and determined intention
can change the winds and time itself.

Listen to the girl.

Stranded on a Rooftop, Shivering

Stranded on a rooftop, shivering, waiting
for rescue while clutching a child;
foul waters below: a flotilla of wreckage—
razor-edged metal, wood ripped away from piers,
twisted, crumpled boats, all manner
of plastics and things that float,
remains of construction sites deconstructed,
split storefronts, dismantled houses,
shingles and screens, disengaged docks,
chunks of causeway lodged against collapsed
steelwork, signage in the days before glitter
of vacationland was violently uprooted
and embedded in dark tempest.

Roofs gone, water gushing in, electrical wires
down, and sweltering cities without power
or light. Hurricane winds reach 400 miles
an hour; sea surge reaches 20 feet, and winds'
penetrating howling hushes the busy. Bodies
in flooded streets: human, animal, bird,
and snapped palm tree rushing in refuse streams
running through communities, over countryside
where waters finally recede, leaving toll
of hurricane in its wake. And the smell—
the hellish stench of decay roiling.

Hurricanes more frequent, storms more violent,
waters breeching ever higher levels as rising
seas make surges more dangerous.
Forty percent of Earth's population lives near a coast.
And the woman and child on the rooftop?
They are clutching one another on the ever-shrinking
rooftop, storm waters swirling below.

When the seas rise, and 3 billion people
are on the move, we will get to know
them climbing closer and closer.

Language like Water

Open mouth, a conduit:
Vowel   owl
flying over; floating in
from rising sea levels—
Assonance tickling in the ear's canal,
consonants descending to depths—
Meaning unbound from strictures of sentence
but not syntax, phonemes then text—
signifier, signified until there is semblance.

Everything sounds like water—
cars rushing past, leaves still attached to limbs,
fan in empty hallway;
passengers on the planet swimming,
drinking, drowning.
Gulping because there is no air for us
beneath surface; balneal, another word for bathing
then diving, way back displaced; undercurrents
in our blood transporting without directive, language
turning and turning serous like Yeats'
ever "widening gyre," we whirl, falling,
splashing, crashing with enough force to sculpt
rock, changing the face of this sphere
far more slowly than our catastrophic
transformations to the oceans.

Relief in the reefs of coral words
and sunken shipwrecked letters;
waterfalls in poetry, of water, under water
orbiting arc through water gardens:
this blue worth fighting for.

To the west of Mariana Islands,
the deepest cut Challenger Deep:
life where no life should exist,
plates mapped out; lakes inside an ocean
alter perception, not magic realism;
new growth as geological strata,
this vocalization of ours eupotamic:
tumbling out of the deepest cut.

Water defying our paltry attempts
to make streets, those aqueous false boundaries
at the limits of backrush;
littoral drift under the influence.

Angle of incidence scarp,
calving at the poles of antithesis;
motion at the bottom caused by density;
Ekman Transport dragging words,
jumbled as they are carried
further from the source.

Estuaries
submerge sounds in incoherence
until born in us again and again,
while we absently forget origins.

Writers write of the sea,
myths and lore diving in anticipation.
Celestine Frost reads ripples,
deciphering codes of "breath sloshing."
We'll find poets at the edge
with those hoping to save the planet.

Here quiet waters ripple, caught by weeds,
insects skim on summer skates;
dragonflies mate on glazing tension,
an angler's flotilla of essays.

What is the speech of water, of history?
Of lakes, seas, rivers, streams?
We hold conch to our ears and imagine
we hear her voice in that enameled chamber.

We become vessels sailing, gliding
until gales arrive. Then we are overturned,
fall into drowning, panic, losing our way
before intuiting our home:
language of incoherence and discovery;

lest we forget: water in our blood,
water, all life's origins.

Corporeal Ghost

Shimmering far below
  water-worn features
  swimming out of long-ago frozen gullies, leaving visible trace:
     imprints in rock until rains
        coursed down,
         down
         down

      where our lungs are aching,
        eardrums bleeding,
    saw-edged spine nearly invisible as it circles round,
   shape neither angel nor devil, wings floating
 on current swells,   embracing
as albino Manta assumes semblance
       of messenger
         at
      periphery:
        aqueous,
      luminous
        kite's warning.

We Had Better Write About Trees

At the edge of the tree line, a sugar maple threatens,
its thick old branches splitting away, hollowed out
in sections where squirrels fought jays for territory.

Further up, a robin laced together precarious nest,
and a finch flew into leaf mass with its pointed lobes.
This old maple showing disaster as the wind picks up,

a break imminent. One limb falls; another echoes,
cracks, and the danger to houses and people below
intensifies, gathering like thunderhead.

Victoria Chang writes, "The Trees Witness Everything,"
and I don't doubt the truth of such personification
any more than the fact we need these behemoths

as living, growing, breaking apart old souls
even as they splinter and crack: a man as tall as a tree,
a woman as wise as an oak, a child as agile as a sapling.

This layering of similes as apt and perilous as our literal
and metaphorical cliffs caused by waiting too long,
looking in the wrong direction to match our greed.

If we each plant a tree, it will not be enough
to make up for the loss of whole forests
when we lack oxygen to breathe.

Adrienne Rich advises, if we want to be heard,
we had better write about trees, its roots
suggestive, its limbs straining to break away,

and the birth and falling of its leaves a reminder
of cyclic renewal even in death, if only we begin
considering ourselves part of this whole.

.

Without Ospreys

For weeks, an osprey perched
on bare branch overlooking shallows.
She preened her feathers,
wide wings stretched and straining
as she focused on ripples made
in minnows' movements,
fish partially hidden by oblique
shadows, clouds covering light.

At odd angles, her wings spread
to dry, before this fish hawk dove,
then flew back to her perch
with prey, still alive but stuck
by her long, curved talons.

From below, distinctive white
underbody streaked with brown
gives her away even
if feather crest on her head
is not yet visible.

What would the Earth be without
the quick, colorful flash of birds?
What would the world's stage be
without judgement of the chorus?

A goldfinch glittering in emerging
sun lands on the branch further out
from osprey, unintimidated
by the predator—no threat to birds.
Osprey whistled as the finch chirped.

When they flew away,
there was such awful absence.

Earth Awakens

In that moment of insight—
silent movement found in descending light—
latecomer coral clouds—
blood-red streaks in the sky—
suggesting another time even another locus
from this far field isolation
with fading tall grasses bent
and blurring figures first,
then thoughts coalescing
into other dark.

That near place—
nearly unreachable now—
once familiar time culled, then held close
from hushed memory
in which distinction is blurred:
the Earth awakens,
our defensive projection,
asking of us,
to what ends?
As we clearcut
another forest,
mine and gouge
for disappearing fossil fuels,
and forget to measure the distance
from plenty to loss.

Examining My Carbon Footprint

Examining the rough soles of my feet,
years into wandering,
I consider high arch, the ball of my foot
that juts out too far, my narrow heel lined
with callouses, and I think of being on my feet
before remembering to ask, what is my carbon footprint?
That CO2 emission I personally
am responsible for, endangering
every lifeform.

I think about waste and chaos,
chaos and waste as the struggle plays out.
I think about politicization and misinformation
told by knowing men as they drill and lie.

I think about trying to reduce or just contain
our wastes or use of electricity, driving my car.

There are enumerated steps to follow
in reducing our dangerously high CO2
emissions, but they are difficult for the individual
to believe that one of us can make any difference
when a single flight uses 36,000 gallons of oil.

Eat less meat, plant a garden, drive less,
waste less—but I'm aware our entire way
of life is based upon manufactured waste
as prime ingredient in profit directive.

Changing how we live so hard when
nearly half the population is still
wrapped and insulated in conspiracies and untruths,
they will never consider science or knowledge
of value. And I think of the generations'
long deceptions by big oil and gas companies—
looking at you, Exxon Mobil, BP, Sinopec,
and Saudi Aramco whose CEOs have duped us all—
with CO2 footprints large enough to fill continents.

When they line up the species to examine
our carbon footprints, none compare to man's
and his legacy of destruction, wars and waste,
what we leave in our wide stance—
small in individual stature, but with CO_2 footprints
of monstrous giants stomping across the land.

But that vision is so dark as to cause giving up
or giving in, so I will do neither and reduce
where I can, when I can and encourage others,
before going out to wild gardens to listen
for the rasping chirp of crickets, the hymn of birds.

We Who Are So Concerned with Death

Folded, nearly unrecognizable, developing wings
expand slowly, ever so slowly within ambiguous
space between life and death. In a hush below
limits of our hearing, pupa impossibly transforms.

With bird-like wings inside layers of silk weavings,
in that interstitial space, in neither death nor sleep,
the Hyalophora Cecropia moth presses itself
through escape valve of the cocoon.
That dry, grey husk looking more like seedling pod
than house of histogenesis in which memory
is not subdued but stored information about leaf
and bough, about timing, about building with silk.

We who are so concerned with death,
scarcely know what to make of this morphing creature;
human beings attempting not to anthropomorphize
but left with incredulity and a need to look beyond.
We have no business projecting upon the cecropia
emerging from its cocoon, but the comparisons
we draw are inescapable, considering the solitude
and severe isolation of the pupa, looking for all
our human senses like a mummified scarab.
When the moth surprises coming from other shores,
we think of its cycle like the caesura in a line.

Then again, this brilliantly colored moth
has no mouth to speak or eat, just a tangle
of lust to breed and lay eggs, beginning again.
In night-full threshold, they take flight,
moths returning to the sky. It is what they do.

It is what we do: project ourselves upon
the natural world, determining the mated pair
of giant moths folding and opening their wings
in desire, no, in love. Magnificent sight of them,
according to mythology of indigenous people,
offer messages from the spirits.
We are silent.

Recalling Blind Beach

No Oedipus stumbling about here at Blind Beach;
rather, dogs—big Black Mouth Curs, fawn-colored
younger pups, descend over perilous rocks,
stone falling away from cliffs to black and gray spectrum of pebbles and finely
broken, empty shells, this changing shoreline where fog and clouds meet,
deceiving the eyes, in this place of concealment near the Russian River outlet
to the sea.

South of Goat Rock, we stand silently in awe of Arch Rock, that offshore
sentry reminding of hidden outcroppings, skerries, and low sea stacks along
Sonoma's coastline.

Get off Highway 1 and follow Goat Rock Road
down its winding, narrow path past sunset boulders from another geologic
age when plate collisions violently gave birth and will again.

No swimming—rip currents disguised:
wild mouth of ocean harboring harbor seals, kelp beds, and fragile
populations of sea life.

Mammoths once tramped and roamed where we stand, where German
Shepherds, Pit Bull Terriers, a pair of Dobermans dominate the stony beach,
dogs leaping over colossal, bleached tree trunks, those skeletal remains of
giants washed up once and left behind, like the Russians
who once logged old growth forest near the river.

Descent to the ocean is difficult; we crawl over what looks like eye-socket of
a leviathan, finding it's only an uprooted redwood, hole left by washed-away
knot of waterlogged wood, but image stays with us as skeletal remains of
another eon we can almost see, no, feel on this stretch of caramel and black
sands along a shifting shoreline remaking itself
again and again
over ages first without,
then with, and
one day without
humankind.

By the Numbers

Bring up the subject of mass extinctions in process, and too many people will blankly stare
as more than a third of all amphibians head out the metaphoric door.

Twenty-one percent of all fish species and reptiles alike are exiting this world without a Pied Piper or discernable sound. Invertebrates are currently leaving at a rate of thirty percent. That means, butterflies, honeybees alarmingly declining, leaving pollination to sustain plant life and our food sources in precarious unbalance. Forty percent of all insects soon to be gone—which does not sound so bad until you reckon with how biodiversity actually works for us all.

Now, here is where the numbers start to hit home: around 90% of primates—our closest relative in the mammalian sphere—live in extinction endangered zones which does not bode well for them or us. Nearly 70% of known plant species are under threat of disappearing, and if that doesn't trouble you, perhaps it is because you were unaware that the oxygen we breathe, the foods we eat, and the medicines we take come largely from plants. By the numbers,
one million species on the way out.

How will the human species fare in this sixth mass extinction?

There will, however, likely be cockroaches, ants, and scorpions setting their bountiful tables
near the shores, and jellyfishication of oceans at the end.

Where Hope Resides

In the midst of crises,
we still have hope.
In a desert without water,
our hope is bottled inside.

In a cave-in after flooding,
hope is a flicker of light
not extinguished until
last breaths, oxygen gone.

In a sinking ship of state,
hope is our last handhold.
In politics rife with hate,
hope resides behind doors.

Irrepressible in the face
of loss and destruction, hope
keeps turning up to wrap
us in essential illusion.

Illusions unless…
we continue to create
new breakthroughs to improve
photosynthesis and wind power.

Continue scientific discoveries
and improve our efficiencies
to better manage our carbon
footprints, and excessive wastes.

We are able to identify
ancestral enzymes at key moments
in history. We can, if we dare,
create solutions for survival.

A Nursery Rhyme Signal

Heat waves and drought,
food supply in doubt,
prices spike as wheat yields fall
while coastal flooding catches the poor in thrall.
Record-breaking weather's disastrous incidence
no longer explained away as coincidence.
Thriving bark and pine beetles decimate forests
while fires ravage miles and miles of forests.
Coral reefs dying; oceans acidifying;
world-wide crises leave no room for denying.

Greed, ignorance, and insolence lead to threatening
new norms of natural catastrophes multiplying,
hurricanes hurling, tornado alleys widening;
fires burning and oceans rising;
greenhouse gas and all kinds of pollutions
for which we have scant solutions.

Have mine canaries stopped singing
their winged warning?

Bodies In Barrels Keep Turning Up

Bodies in barrels keep turning up
on cracked and dry reservoir bed.
Waters recede as climate change forms
new deserts and expands old ones,
humans tipping the balance
even in formation of the Sahara.

Earth is rebelling from misuse:
our trash ubiquitous, soiling air and water
as if they were as infinite as space;
cars and generators vomit CO_2
while development pushes boundaries
past limits and forests are clearcut.

Commercial flight burning 36,000 gallons
of oil while we run out of resources,
clean water, and even sands disappearing.
Oil and gas violently extracted from below
as we dredge the seafloor,
dump our wastes, altering land and oceans;
we burn and drain peatlands
which hold dangerous carbon.
We pollute and pollute and pollute
with human and animal waste,
with pesticides, with poisonous demands,
depleting and degrading even the soil.
We harvest natural gas
and precipitate earthquakes,
destroy coral reefs, and burn fossil fuels
that are dangerously warming Natura.

Those bodies in barrels our reminder:
we have not been good guardians.
Aquifers are receding,
yet we sip our lattes and debate
how long we have known.

No wonder we look to the stars
and talk about cheap flights to Mars.

Discordant Chorus

Sculptor forcing proximity of seeming light and dark,
a confession of illusory opposites—
the impossibility of soft hardness of woven wooden figures
as art on a wall.

Not at all what they seem because lines in wood speak
of relationships born in ancient origins and ending stories,
in the remains of trees signaling other eons in geologic time,
now reproduced as metaphors coming into concordance—

this discordant chorus of ageless,
visionary voices
unable to speak our language,
yet we know; we must know.

A River Still Runs Through It

With the Mississippi River, the mighty Mississippi,
nature has a way of opening wounds inflicted
by man as the river dries up and ships, one built
in the 1800s, are exposed. Bones, once sideboards,
looking like ribcage of ancient Goliath
uncovered along with discarded oil drums,
plastic bottles and plastic everything.

Vessels run aground due to low water levels,
a queue of barges and boats stuck in muck.
A massive island in the middle of the river,
Tower Rock becomes tourist hotspot as throngs
walk across what was once swirling river
with not a second thought about old gods;
stretches of the riverbed looking more
like desert. Buoy used to help boats navigate
becomes stranded along shore, tangled in
discarded ropes and mounds of rusting wire.

Color palette has changed: once blue,
our rivers run painted with yellows, greens,
and browns as fertilizer runoffs from agribusiness
and climate change test the limits of artists'
and water's ability to create. Toxic green
Algae blooms thriving, bubbling up from
this caldron of nasty brew.

Too many rivers going "biologically dead,"
even as sawdust dumps and blood and guts
from slaughterhouses lessen impact,
fertilizers take their place running
into rivers. Wastewater treatment discharge
and pharmaceutical pollution reign.

Human thoughtlessness and greed—
all the evidence we need.

Arbiter of Justice

No bare breast nor submission here,
Nemesis is forever proud and fierce,
wearing her long robes and wide wings
as any fierce goddess is intended.

Our personification designed for those who commit evil,
this Greek goddess goes about exacting revenge,
for we know without justice, without an accounting
of wrongs, there can be no peace.

Nemesis is, in short, Hell to pay.
Existing on another plane in which injustices
are laid bare and summarily dealt with.
This goddess is sure of herself without rhetoric.

Daughter of Oceanus or Zeus,
perhaps Nyx, the origins of Nemesis
less certain than her unholy mood
as she enacts vengeance and retribution.

Like blind Lady Justice,
she is often blindfolded, feeling
man's injuries to Earth, man not seeing
his responsibility.

Quite literally, her name
means to give what is due. Ruthless
but unfailing in her certainty of right,
Nemesis wields her sword.

Hope for Water Bears

At the furthest edges of human destruction,
we have calm of the water bear,
perhaps the most indestructible species on our planet.

This eight-legged micro-animal
is believed to have survived cataclysm and will likely
withstand our own apocalyptic endings—
surviving everything, really, except an extinguished sun.

"Moss piglets," or Tardigrade,
if you want to get scientific with naming, but it's likely
water bears don't care much for nomenclature,
humans, or their affairs.

Water bears aren't very strong, but they can endure
a trip into outer space on the skin of a rocket ship
out and back again through fiery atmosphere.
Only around 10 billion years of drawing in water
and lasting through dehydration in their desiccation state,
reminiscent of hibernation,
water bears are all about coming through.
No food or water for thirty years? They endure.

Not terribly attractive, water bears resemble
an Idaho potato gone soft, sprouting tiny claws.
Or looking like miniature moles with rhino hide—
they have long, sunken slits where eyes would be
but are not likely to care about
our estimations of their beauty
as they burrow in the lowest parts of seas
or attach to highest mountains.

If we only speak of humanities' love,
our art, music, and quest for knowledge,
we might mistakenly pity the water bear.

**Birdlike Bones
and Other Assorted Similes**

We compare ourselves to animals: strong as a bull,
the simile, before saying, "He has a heart like a lion."

Although we seldom hear, "He has the face
of an orangutang," it feels apt, once in a while,
to compare countenances with one of our closest
mammalian relatives because we are all relatives,
and our family tree is not nearly as straight
and is far more diverse than we like to admit
while disparaging others and carelessly
or purposefully slaughtering species.

D.H. Lawrence went so far as to help us see
ourselves in a "Baby Tortoise." Elizabeth Bishop
had us at "The Armadillo" in which we are unmasked
as ignorant against night sky.

Our animal metaphors come back to haunt us
as half of all species are projected to be extinct
by the end of the century in which our planet beckons
to us to find solutions to the great crises we,
as self-anointed mini-Gods, have rained down.

Last Light

Against high, barren backdrop,
like an unholy Trinity in the rain,
three shapes of dark matter

hunched, not perched
in the way of spring birds,
but squatted, sullen and unkept,

with discontented plumage
jagged as invisible wings fold
into themselves, disappearing

any thought of flight;
their talons dug into barren snag,
exposing brown, dry inner layer

of a tree not dormant and leafless,
limbs no longer in distress,
but clean-stripped of bark.

These shades from another realm,
seeming totems of death,
were formed in the human mind,

perhaps foreshadowing; nevertheless,
their massive bodies never moved,
and their eyes followed my approach

as if granting this short extension.
"I will see you again," I whispered
before hurrying on my way.

Things the Water Carried

On an ordinary day, you venture
outside, walk the shoreline to find
bloated carp arrived upside down,
plastic bag breathing in and out
in the sunlight, twisted clear
container that once held food,
a rusting bicycle cast off
or stolen in another lifetime,
cans and bottles form an entity,
plastics strangling plastics,
a whitened, barkless tree limb
resembling slender arm.

Moving out past the coasts,
the Great Pacific garbage patch—
human refuse bound by North Pacific
subtropical gyre—
these microplastics as boundless
as human intentions.
Within one clump: toy green soldier,
cell phone, Batman mask, lighter,
fishing gear, shoes, needles,
all manmade oddities held together
by synthetic, fishermen's nets.
How much is there? NOAA
estimates cleanup of this island
of garbage would take 67 ships
a year to remove this peculiar island
from its North Pacific home.

Returning to shores of an inland lake,
Styrofoam containers gleam,
white skin wrapped by red rope
attached to matted, graying bird
missing an eye: clash
between the natural world
and the one we have created.

Beyond the mountaintops,
rumblings widen, vibrations
of distant storms closing in.

When the World Was Young

        I

When the world was young
energy passed through water.

When the world was young,
violent collisions saw beginnings born
of endings, and cyanobacteria set the stage
for transformations into multicellular life.

When the world was young, microbes
formed on hard structures. Sponges
and fronds proliferated in the seas until
the Cambrian Period saw paroxysms
of lifeforms with hard and soft body
parts, spines and protective shells.

When the world was still very young,
oceans retreated and land masses
formed from volcanic eruptions,
plants colonized the land, and a flowering
began as life came crawling out
of water, with webs emerging
in which one species found another,
interdependent for survival.

        II

When the World is no longer young,
walking at the changing tide line, an avocet
approaches a hermit crab tucking itself
into its new home. A starfish is washed back
into the sea with a wave, out beyond
the breakers, a pelican dives and fills
its gular with fish, tails still sticking out
of its wide, grinning bill.

When the world is no longer young,
two men rip away a pelican's

gullet and jam it over the bird's head,
beavers are skinned and carcasses tossed,
dogfighting rings, cock fighting betting,
common cruelty practiced by man.

When the world is no longer young,
dolphins and whales are herded
into blood-red coves in Taiji, Japan,
in annual slaughter.

When the world is no longer young, humans,
just 0.01% of living things, caused the loss
of 83% of all wild animals and plant life.

When the world is no longer young,
human ignorance, greed, and disregard

are bringing about one outcome.

Aliens

Not out of some horror movie
but from the natural world,
acids of lichen turn stone to soil,
and another look at lichen has us
discovering they are made up of over
120 species of fungi and bacteria.

So, not a single living organism
after all, and like coral that is not one
entity but comprised of anemone-like
animals called polyps; or take
the Portuguese Man of War
that is actually a colony of zooids.

Finding its way along the bottom
of the world, the spotted salamander, too,
has a symbiotic relationship with algae.

When it comes to composite entities, we
think "alien," until discovering we, as well,
are those aliens offering a microbiome
landscape, each of us, if each is even
an operable word to describe the human
home to 39 trillion microbial cells

of bacteria, viruses, and fungi.
So, it turns out, alien is the right word.
We are all made of Stardust.

Once Fallen on Earth

When we turn
                to visions of our escape
from a scorching planet
                on an imagined silver spaceship heading out
                          into an indifferent universe,
        our fantasies take hold,
              as we breathe a sigh of relief,
                      and we travel far from our beleaguered home
but fail to lament a moaning man in the moon
                        and weeping wild Earth, this beautiful sphere
                            knowing her lost children
are heading for the brightest star,
                      but Sirius burned itself out long
                      before we are due to arrive
                            as cosmic dust.

**Halfway Between Center and Edge,
in a Galaxy Called the Milky Way**

Seven million miles from Earth,
beyond even BepiColombo's satellite
images, a giant space rock circles
an asteroid. Irregular in shape, coal-black,
a mixture of metals formed in violent
collisions, named Dimorphos for its duality,
this moon orbits its own sphere
hurtling through expanding space.

Such introduction could have come at the beginning of a disaster movie, but this scenario starred engineers, technicians, and physicists working in labs to alter perception and intercept a moving target in the first successful interplanetary defense system test.

At the edge of our anxiety about life,
at the far reaches of even our technology,
there is yet hope. This kernel of potential
comes not from empty words and gestures,
not from boasts or boundless deceit
but human ingenuity, creativity,
persistence, and doggedly good science
all working together to achieve a goal.

If we can alter the course of Dimorphos seven million miles away and avert a potential threat to the planet (even one not really a threat), we can relearn to clean up our waste, conserve our fuel, lower our carbon footprint: what is possible has become what is crucial.

We may still become that strange, compelling
species writing symphonies and building towers—
symbolically, metaphorically, and literally—
in harmony on this most remarkable blue orb
halfway between the center and furthest edges
of our Milky Way Galaxy, an Earth
teaming with diverse and extraordinary
creatures in delicate, beautiful balance.

Author and educator **Nancy Avery Dafoe** writes across genres and has won multiple awards for her work, including the William Faulkner/William Wisdom creative writing competition in poetry (2016). She won first place in the international short story competition from New Century Writers and first prize in prose poetry from the Soul-Making Literary competition, among other honors for her work. Dafoe has fourteen published books, including her four collections of poetry (FLP), the most recent before this chapbook being *The House Was Quiet, But the Mind Was Anxious*. She recently had a memoir published about the loss of her son, *Unstuck in Time: A Memoir and Mystery on Loss and Love* (Pen Women Press, 2021), and her most recent novel *Socrates is Dead Again* (PWP, 2022) is literary fiction. Dafoe has also written about her mother's Alzheimer's and its effect on the family in her memoir *An Iceberg in Paradise: A Passage Through Alzheimer's* (SUNY Press, 2015). Her contemporary fable/novella *Naimah and Ajmal on Newton's Mountain* (FLP) joins her other fiction work: three mystery novels, *You Enter a Room, Both End in Speculation,* and *Murder on Ponte Vecchio* (RPP). Her poetry books include *The House Was Quiet, But the Mind Was Anxious* (FLP, 2022); *Innermost Sea;* and *Poets Diving in the Night* (FLP). In addition, Dafoe has written books on educational policy and teaching writing, published through Rowman & Littlefield Education: *Breaking Open the Box, The Misdirection of Education Policy,* and *Writing Creatively.*

Her fiction, poetry, and nonfiction works appear in a number of anthologies, including *Lost Orchard* (SUNY Press) and *Lost Orchard II* (PWP); *NY Votes for Women: A Suffrage Centennial Anthology* (Cayuga Lake Books); *Birdsong; Earth Care: Environment Problems and Possible Solutions; From the Finger Lakes, a Memoir Anthology,* and in numerous journals and magazines.

Dafoe has taught English and writing in a variety of settings, including high school, community college, and workshops. She continues to offer writing workshops through a variety of settings and may be contacted through her websites: nancydafoebooks.com. She is a member of the National League of American Pen Women (NLAPW) and Central New York (CNY) Branch.

She and her husband Daniel live in Homer, New York.

www.ingramcontent.com/pod-product-compliance
Lightning Source LLC
Chambersburg PA
CBHW022149180426
43200CB00028BA/496